DEGREE OF
PERSISTENCE

120 TIPS TO FINISH YOUR DOCTORATE WITHOUT LOSING YOUR MIND

DR. KESSLYN

TO: _____

FROM: _____

DEGREE OF
PERSISTENCE

120 TIPS TO FINISH YOUR DOCTORATE WITHOUT LOSING YOUR MIND

DR. KESSLYN

This book is dedicated to all those doctoral pursuers who have spent time and energy to complete the doctoral degree in order to make a dynamic difference in the world.

Acknowledgements

Any success that I have can be attributed to the inspiration of my grandparents, the influence of my parents, the example of my brother, the love of my children, the support of my closest friends, the persistence of my ancestors, the presence of doctoral pursuers, and the power of God, who paved the way for me to complete this journey. Thank you.

DEGREE OF PERSISTENCE

I have my dream job. I love being a social work educator, and I must be pretty good at it because I've received coveted teaching awards, speaking awards and have been promoted to Full Professor. And best of all, I now can leverage my knowledge, values, and skills to make a dynamic difference in the world.

I truly do love my job!

But the journey from small town girl to college professor was not easy. In fact, one of the most difficult parts was pursuing the doctoral degree. The journey was not necessarily difficult because of the course work. I'd been a great student through my three other degree programs, so academics were not an issue. Additionally, I had previously published articles and had presented at numerous conferences before I had been accepted into the doctoral program, so writing and clarity about messaging were not problematic, either.

No, the difficulties of my doctoral journey stemmed from a lack of inspiration and information about the doctoral journey. There were times when the loneliness and feelings of being stuck seemed insurmountable, and while my family was supportive, they didn't understand the doctoral journey. At a certain point, I really thought I was going to lose my mind! As a result, I spent many more years than necessary on a quest to achieve the degree that has solidified the current fulfillment of my dream career.

After I graduated, I took some time to recoup. What was clear to me was the thought that I didn't want people to go through that same isolating, financially stressful process that I had just come out of. So, I asked myself, "what can I do to fill the gap and help other emerging scholars?" My response was to voluntarily offer support to doctoral students and doctoral candidates. Well, that voluntary work evolved into an entrepreneurial enterprise designed to enable doctoral pursuers to get in, through, and out of their doctoral programs.

It has been nearly 10 years now that I have been supporting other doctoral pursuers, and I have learned quite a bit. Thanks to my own experiences and those shared by my clients and doctoral friends, I now have a collection of "tips" that will help address the mental, emotional, financial, and relational strain that can assault and assail those in doctoral programs.

I know what you are saying. "Who needs ANOTHER book to read?" That was my thought, too! So, instead of providing another "dense" book to read that may feel like another stressful task, I designed this book as an easy read to share helpful hints for your success. No matter what page you read, you will easily be informed and inspired regarding specific categories: mindset, self-care, finances, doctoral logistics, and relationships.

My goal is to provide practical support. No, this easy read does not provide you with all of the answers, but it is a good cheat-sheet to use for your doctoral success. The book also includes space at the end of each section for you to write. Use this space to jot down ways that you can include the hints in your own doctoral journey. Use the space to dream. Use the space to plan. Use the space to reflect. Use the space to propel you forward!

This simple read packs a lot of practical value for those who are on the doctoral journey. Use it so you can earn your degree without losing your mind. ENJOY!

STRUGGLES & STRAINS

Struggles and Strains

When I entered my doctoral program twenty years ago, I fully intended to leave in three to four years with a doctoral degree. Instead, it took me seven. And when I had finished, I was lost and lonely. It seemed as if the process had stripped me of all that I had known about myself, others and the academy. I had given up so much and seemingly lost so much more, including full-time employment, financial stability, intimate relationships, friendships, and my own mental well-being.

I wish I had known then what I know now about the struggles that doctoral students face. At least I would not have thought I was "the only one". What I now know is that most doctoral pursuers face challenges of some sort while in the program. These challenges may vary by size and significance, but all the struggles have the potential to derail doctoral scholars.

As any good researcher would do, I wanted to know that my experiences and observations were not just my own. So, in an effort to explore whether my perceptions about those struggles were accurate, I leveraged social media and made note of the issues that doctoral students and doctoral candidates encountered. I found that many doctoral scholars encounter issues related to mindset, self-care, finances, relationships, and logistics surrounding the doctoral process. Here are some of the most consistent struggles that I saw.

- Personal physical and mental health

- Academic hazing

- Lack of personal support, patience, and humility

- Procrastination

- Isolation after the completion of classes

- Imposter Syndrome

STRUGGLES & **STRAINS**

- Burnout

- School/Life balance

- Dissertation writing

- Lack of mentoring

- Low confidence

- Limited support for topics of interest

- Bureaucracy within the university

- Limited interest in research on people of color

- Disagreements between committee members

- Unclear program policies and practices

- Time management

- Financial constraints

- Writing inefficiencies

- No motivation

- Dissolution of marriage while in the program

- Having children while in the program

- Limited cultural competence and cultural humility within programs

- Extended time in program due to inaccurate academic advising

Unfortunately, many of these challenges lead to larger compounding issues that have an impact on one's well-being, beyond the doctoral program itself. While some doctoral pursuers have chosen to cope with the challenges in healthy ways, others have chosen unhealthy coping strategies and formed addictions that overshadow the path toward doctoral completion. Some doctoral

STRUGGLES & STRAINS

seekers have acknowledged gaining and losing drastic amounts of weight, developing drinking and drug habits, and having suicidal ideations due to the stress and loneliness associated with the doctoral journey.

In the next few pages, I have provided some helpful hints to support you through the journey. Use them. Write them down. Refer to them often. Repeat them as a mantra for your success. Implement them to help you manage milestone achievement along the path to your ultimate destiny.

NOTES & REFLECTIONS

NOTES & REFLECTIONS

MINDSET MATTERS

Mindset Matters

In order to succeed in a doctoral program, one must recognize that your mental positioning, also known as "mindset", makes a substantial impact on your success. This segment of the book will provide you with some helpful hints about how to position your mind for this doctoral journey.

1. Be true to yourself.

2. Write down your "why", because it will motivate you when your "what" may not.

3. Remind yourself that the journey itself is just as important as the destination, especially when the doctoral journey

DEGREE OF PERSISTENCE

feels more like academic hazing.

4. Engage in the doctoral process with a spirit of inquiry that will eventually lead to innovation.

5. Maintain your integrity. Sometimes, it may be the only thing that you have.

6. Know your personal strengths and operate from them.

7. Develop and repeat a personal daily mantra that reiterates who you are, with or without the doctoral degree.

8. Don't transform into an image that is not representative of the essence of who you

MINDSET MATTERS

are and who you desire to be.

9.   Embrace personal change as a result of the doctoral journey, and become an even greater life-long learner.

10. Remember to nourish your soul. When the soul is nurtured, the mind and body will operate at a higher standard.

11. Recognize that your resolve will be tested by life itself, but it will also take you through the rocky terrain and across the finish line.

12. Function like the doctoral journey is a marathon that is run at your own pace. Drop the "sprint" mentality.

13. Prepare yourself for the process of discovery. The guidelines are sometimes clear and unclear, simultaneously.

14. Know that everyone's doctoral journey is unique and different; yet, the only people who may understand this are those who have gone through the doctoral process.

15. Remember that no matter how well-regarded you are in other spheres, while on the doctoral journey you are a student who is preparing to become an expert scholar-practitioner. Remain humble.

16. Be the student who seeks assistance and asks questions.

MINDSET MATTERS

17. Recognize that Imposter Syndrome is REAL and is common for many who are along the doctoral journey.

18. Marry your personal confidence and humility.

19. Remember that you have already been accepted into the program because of the amazing strengths and skills that you possess.

20. Stay grounded and realistic.

21. Relax and trust the process. It happens the way that it is supposed to.

DEGREE OF PERSISTENCE

22. Know your personal challenges, especially those that have the potential to transform into a habit that could threaten your success.

23. Keep being courageous and know that you are getting your doctorate because your "why" is guiding your "what".

24. When things get difficult and you feel like stopping the journey, ask yourself the following: "Stop and do what?"

25. You may feel like quitting.   Don't! Refuse to quit!

26. It doesn't matter when you start or how long it takes; what matters is that you finish.

NOTES & REFLECTIONS

NOTES & REFLECTIONS

NOTES & REFLECTIONS

DEGREE OF PERSISTENCE

SELF-CARE & SACRIFICES

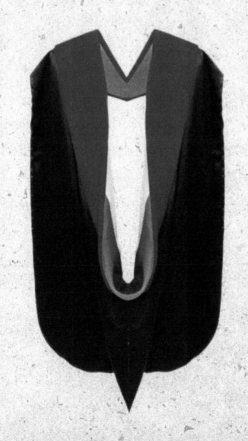

Self-Care and Sacrifices

It has been said that graduate students suffer from depression and anxiety at a rate that is much higher than the general population. And as many know, both anxiety and depression can have a significant impact on one's progress toward goal attainment.

This segment provides you with some helpful self-care strategies as a way to help you combat anxiety, depression, and other challenges, before and during their onset.

27.   Remember that you are worth caring for.

28.   Provide maintenance for your holistic being.

29.   Maintain all of your medical appointments.

30.   Nurture your spiritual life by practicing at least one spiritual activity daily (e.g. meditation, prayer, yoga, candle lighting,

spiritual reading, etc.).

31. Utilize your "Hour of Power" first thing in the morning: 20 minutes of meditation, 20 minutes of reading, and 20 minutes of outlining the plans for the day.

32. Keep a schedule and calendar for all important events.

33. Mark time on your schedule for regular rest and relaxation (e.g. daily cup of tea, weekly time away from work, monthly grooming appointment, quarterly staycation, annual family vacation).

34. Exercise at least 30 minutes, three times per week.

35. Eat as many whole foods as possible, rather than processed foods.

36. Take at least two 15-minute time-outs throughout every day to stretch and connect

SELF CARE & SACRIFICES

with yourself and others.

37. Develop a paid and/or volunteer support system (e.g. nanny, housekeeper, editor, writing groups, etc.) to help you address issues that are stressful for you.

38. Utilize virtual communities to ask and answer questions.

39. Celebrate the large and small wins.

40. Develop and utilize a daily schedule so that life can be as "automated" as possible.

41. Repeat your personal mantra at least once per day.

42. Work hard, play hard, and relax often.

NOTES & REFLECTIONS

NOTES & REFLECTIONS

NOTES & REFLECTIONS

NOTES & REFLECTIONS

FINANCIAL FITNESS

Financial Fitness

Did you know that finance is listed as one of the top 10 stressors for doctoral pursuers? And while I believe that programs that want you to pursue your doctoral degree with them should provide financial support, many do not. Instead, far too many doctoral pursuers are left to creatively devise their own plans for financing their degree and their lifestyle.

This section of the book provides some considerations for how you can do just that. Yes, being in a doctoral program means that you must re-evaluate your finances and livelihood, but these tips are provided to help you.

43. Know your own worth.

44. Recognize that an investment in yourself now will produce financial dividends later.

45. Become meticulous when it comes to income and expenses.

46. Save as much as you can prior to beginning your doctoral program.

47. Identify and implement methods that provide passive income and require less investment of your time.

48. Develop a financial strategy that will sustain you and your family before you begin your doctoral program.

49. Re-evaluate your financial strategy monthly, quarterly, and annually to measure effectiveness and to consider adjustments.

50. Live with an "essentials only" mentality before starting your program so that the financial adjustments required while in school may not feel as drastic.

51. Challenge yourself to continue living on a minimalist's budget once you enter your program.

52. Remember to schedule and use each of the 168 hours allotted per week to your advantage so you don't waste time and money.

53. Request financial support from your university during your admissions process. If they want you to be there, they should invest in you.

54. Work on grant-funded research while in your doctoral degree program. This will develop you experientially and economically.

55. Supplement your income by serving as an adjunct professor.

56. Utilize all educational benefits provided by your employer, including alternative work schedules, tuition remission, and leave time.

57. Consider securing employment or engaging in volunteer opportunities (e.g. Residence Hall Director or Chaplain-in-Residence) that can defray one of life's major expenses, such as housing, transportation and/or food.

58. Embrace the opportunity to be a Graduate Assistant, Teaching Assistant or Research Assistant, because they will enhance your set of skills and supplement your income.

59. Write grants that will "buy your time" and connect with your research interests. Be sure to include funding for assistants who can support your doctoral research endeavors.

FINANCIAL FITNESS

60. Ask about funding opportunities that may be provided by foundations and educational trusts.

61. Consider being a Fulbright Scholar or a Rhodes Scholar.

62. Inquire about funding opportunities for doctoral pursuers through your professional organizations and civic groups.

63. Do not take out student loans unless you absolutely must.

64. If you must take out a student loan, consider using it to invest in items that will appreciate and provide long-term financial stability (e.g. a home) versus wasting it on purchases that provide temporary creature comfort but will depreciate immediately after purchase (e.g. clothes or a car).

65. Don't pay rent on loaned money.

66. Prepare for internship and licensure processes, which can both be expensive.

67. Invest in great equipment, including but not limited to a great laptop, a printer/scanner, an electronic stapler, a three-hole punch, a reference indexing system, paper, paper clips, etc.

68. Stock up on school supplies during the sale and clearance seasons.

69. Become a member of professional organizations that provide student discounts.

NOTES & REFLECTIONS

DEGREE OF PERSISTENCE

NOTES & REFLECTIONS

NOTES & REFLECTIONS

DEGREE OF PERSISTENCE

LATITUDE OF LOGISTICS

™

Latitude of Logistics

Many people have considered becoming a doctor, but don't know where to start. Of those who do begin by completing the application, only 15% are admitted, in some cases. Furthermore, of those who are admitted, only 50% successfully complete their degrees, and many of them do so after spending more time in their program than they initially expected. Why?

Well, in order to make it through the doctoral program successfully, without wasting money and time, one must have a plan that is based on logistical knowledge. This section is designed to provide you with some knowledge and strategies to help you successfully complete your program without wasting time and money.

70. Keep It Simple, Scholar. (Translation: Don't overthink it.)

71. Organize your life so that as much of it as possible can run on auto-pilot.

72. Your work does not have to be perfect; just perfectible through further future research.

73. Recognize that the doctoral journey is an exercise that teaches you how to conduct research for practice and not one that expects you to be a perfected researcher.

74. Surround yourself with a network of coaches, consultants, and scholars who can provide you with wisdom about navigating the process.

75. Utilize a productivity or accountability partner to keep you on track.

76. Take as many supplemental classes as possible, including some in business and entrepreneurship, that may be beneficial

toward the attainment of your future goals.

77. Set personal limits and deadlines.

78. Begin the doctoral program with some sense of your dissertation topic, even if it is very broad.

79. Become familiar with the format of each chapter as well as the guidelines for your university and school.

80. Complete every assignment and write every paper on a subject that is related to your dissertation topic.

81. Utilize a reference indexing and management system from the very first day of class to keep sources organized.

82. Keep an annotated bibliography of every article that you read.   The annotated bibliography should include the name of the

author, name of the article, date of publication, name of the journal, theoretical framework, type of article, variables of the study, research methods, research question(s), findings, strengths, and limitations.

83. Remember that your Literature Review is designed to report what is already known and highlight what needs to be discovered.

84. Start writing your literature review as early as possible, even if the details and structure change over time.

85. Synthesize the literature by comparing and contrasting what is known and what is not known across all of the related articles.

86. Use categories to help you synthesize the literature, including variables, methods, theories, participants, findings, limitations,

and recommendations.

87. Remember that your goal as a researcher is to fill the gaps in the data that exists. Your literature review helps you identify the gaps, your research questions formally acknowledge the gaps, your methodology provides the roadmap for getting answers for the gaps, your findings fill the gaps, and your recommendations tell others what to do with the gaps once filled.

88. When considering your recruitment and sampling method for participants, think seriously about who you already have access to and how easily you can access them.

89. When thinking about doing secondary data analysis, consider the data to which you already have access.

90. Get an interpreter when data analysis seems daunting and your data seems indiscernible.

91. Submit drafts to your advisor on a regular basis, whether requested or not.

92. Choose committee members who are invested in your success, have the time to meet with you, and get along with others on the committee, as evidenced by the success rates of other graduates from your program.

93. Embrace the opportunity to expand your research capabilities and don't let fear of qualitative or quantitative research lead you away from it.

94. Schedule regular meetings with your advisor and members of your committee to discuss next steps, to receive feedback, and to get clarity.

LATITUDE OF LOGISTICS

95. Inquire often and be open to the feedback.

96. Use your "breaks" to participate in writing groups and accountability groups so you don't "lose steam". You must keep writing.

97. Keep a running list of recommendations, the dates for the recommendations, the person who made the recommendation, and how/where it was addressed.

98. Save and date EVERY VERSION of your document and maintain a "scraps" file to refer back to, in the event that you need to include it in a later version. NOTE: Don't permanently delete anything.

99. Begin writing your IRB proposal(s) as your methodology becomes clear. Then finalize it after your proposal has been approved, so you can send it out for approval. NOTE: The IRB approval process can be lengthy

and tedious.

100. If you get stuck or need clarity, ask your Chair/Advisor for a timeline.

101. Get a good editor and know that good editors cost good money.

102. Check originality before submitting your final draft.

103. Write and publish at least three articles from your dissertation.

104. A good dissertation is a done dissertation. That does not require perfection; just persistence.

NOTES & REFLECTIONS

DEGREE OF PERSISTENCE

NOTES & REFLECTIONS

NOTES & REFLECTIONS

DEGREE OF PERSISTENCE

REALITIES OF
RELATIONSHIPS

Realities of Relationships

Relationships are important for everyone, but they can both evolve and devolve very easily for those who are along the doctoral journey. In fact, before entering my own doctoral program, I heard that 50% of all marriages end while doctoral seekers are in doctoral programs. I recognize that these statistics are on par with the average divorce rates in the United States, but I can't help but wonder if the academic rigors of the doctoral journey exacerbate pre-existing marital challenges and introduce others. And I know from personal experience that other intimate relationships can suffer as well, during doctoral programs, making it an even more daunting and lonely journey.

The reality is that relationships are important and must be handled with care by doctoral pursuers. They can directly and indirectly impact the time and degree of your doctoral success. Here are a few tips to consider regarding relationships during the doctoral process.

105. Set strong, clear, and consistent boundaries.

106. Embrace those relationships that nourish you.

107. Understand that your relationships will shift while you are pursuing your doctoral degree.

108. Build your support network with people inside and outside the academy.

109. Develop "teammate" relationships with your cohort and grow together if you can, but also remember that sometimes team sports require individual successes.

110. Every member of your cohort may not be "your kind of people" but everyone has something of value to bring to the table.

REALITIES OF RELATIONSHIPS

111. Remember that after classes are completed, the dissertation writing phase can be very isolating, so having a coach who understands you and the process is very beneficial.

112. Recognize that everyone has challenges and everyone has strengths; build accordingly.

113. Release those who have demonstrated that they are not aligned with your values, vision, dreams, goals, and forward movement, even if the release is temporary.

114. Be aware of the politics within higher education and doctoral programs, and steer clear by avoiding taking sides.

115. Build relationships with others through online doctoral communities.

116. Have at least one great doctoral coach, mentor/advisor, counselor/therapist,

statistician, and spiritual leader on your personal team.

117. Remember that the most important relationship to maintain during the doctoral process is the one between you and God.

118. Manage your expectations of others who have not gone through the doctoral process. They may never understand the mental, physical, spiritual, emotional, psychological, and financial sacrifices and investments that you have made to get where you are.

119. Remember that the doctoral degree is not merely a degree of intelligence; it is a degree of persistence!

120. PERSIST!

NOTES & REFLECTIONS

DEGREE OF PERSISTENCE

NOTES & REFLECTIONS

NOTES & REFLECTIONS

DEGREE OF PERSISTENCE

NOTES & REFLECTIONS

NOTES & REFLECTIONS

DEGREE OF PERSISTENCE

NOTES & REFLECTIONS

DEGREE OF PERSISTENCE

BONUS JOURNAL

TO MAINTAIN YOUR PERSISTENCE

The following pages are designed to help you plan and implement your weekly goals for the year.

ANTICIPATE A NEW REALITY

Jan   Feb   Mar   April   May   June   July   Aug   Sept   Oct   Nov   Dec
1 2 3 4 5 6 7 8 9 10 11 12 13 14 15 16 17 18 19 20 21 22 23 24 25 26 27 28 29 30

DREAM

TO DO

GOALS

ACCOMPLISHMENTS

WEEK 1 OBJECTIVES

_____

_____

_____

_____

_____

NEXT STEPS

OBSTACLES & SOLUTIONS

DEGREE OF PERSISTENCE

www.DrKesslyn.com

BELIEVE

DREAM

TO DO

GOALS

ACCOMPLISHMENTS

WEEK 1 OBJECTIVES

_____
_____
_____
_____
_____
_____

NEXT STEPS

OBSTACLES & SOLUTIONS

DEGREE OF PERSISTENCE
www.DrKesslyn.com

CONSIDER YOUR "WHY"

Jan   Feb   Mar   April   May   June   July   Aug   Sept   Oct   Nov   Dec
1 2 3 4 5 6 7 8 9 10 11 12 13 14 15 16 17 18 19 20 21 22 23 24 25 26 27 28 29 30

DREAM

TO DO

GOALS

ACCOMPLISHMENTS

WEEK 1 OBJECTIVES

_____
_____
_____
_____
_____

NEXT STEPS

OBSTACLES & SOLUTIONS

REAM ABOUT THE "WHAT"

Jan   Feb   Mar   April   May   June   July   Aug   Sept   Oct   Nov   Dec
3 4 5 6 7 8 9 10 11 12 13 14 15 16 17 18 19 20 21 22 23 24 25 26 27 28 29 30 31

REAM

TO DO

OALS

ACCOMPLISHMENTS

VEEK 1 OBJECTIVES

_____

_____

_____

_____

_____

NEXT STEPS

OBSTACLES & SOLUTIONS

DEGREE OF PERSISTENCE

EXPLORE YOUR OPTIONS

Jan   Feb   Mar   April   May   June   July   Aug   Sept   Oct   Nov   Dec
1 2 3 4 5 6 7 8 9 10 11 12 13 14 15 16 17 18 19 20 21 22 23 24 25 26 27 28 29 30

DREAM

TO DO

GOALS

ACCOMPLISHMENTS

WEEK 1 OBJECTIVES

_____
_____
_____
_____
_____

NEXT STEPS

OBSTACLES & SOLUTIONS

DEGREE OF PERSISTENCE
www.DrKesslyn.com

FIGURE OUT A PLAN

Jan   Feb   Mar   April   May   June   July   Aug   Sept   Oct   Nov   Dec
2 3   4   5   6   7   8   9   10 11 12 13 14 15 16 17 18 19 20 21 22 23 24 25 26 27 28 29 30 31

DREAM

TO DO

GOALS

ACCOMPLISHMENTS

WEEK 1 OBJECTIVES

_____

_____

_____

_____   **NEXT STEPS**

_____

OBSTACLES & SOLUTIONS

GARNER SUPPORT

Jan	Feb	Mar	April	May	June	July	Aug	Sept	Oct	Nov	Dec

1 2 3 4 5 6 7 8 9 10 11 12 13 14 15 16 17 18 19 20 21 22 23 24 25 26 27 28 29 30

DREAM

TO DO

GOALS

ACCOMPLISHMENTS

WEEK 1 OBJECTIVES

_____
_____
_____
_____

NEXT STEPS

_____

OBSTACLES & SOLUTIONS

DEGREE OF PERSISTENCE

www.DrKesslyn.com

HONOR YOUR LEGACY

Jan   Feb   Mar   April   May   June   July   Aug   Sept   Oct   Nov   Dec
2 3 4 5 6 7 8 9 10 11 12 13 14 15 16 17 18 19 20 21 22 23 24 25 26 27 28 29 30 31

REAM

TO DO

GOALS

ACCOMPLISHMENTS

WEEK 1 OBJECTIVES

_____
_____
_____
_____
_____

NEXT STEPS

OBSTACLES & SOLUTIONS

DEGREE OF PERSISTENCE

INITIATE THE DREAM

Jan	Feb	Mar	April	May	June	July	Aug	Sept	Oct	Nov	Dec

1 2 3 4 5 6 7 8 9 10 11 12 13 14 15 16 17 18 19 20 21 22 23 24 25 26 27 28 29 30

DREAM

TO DO

GOALS

ACCOMPLISHMENTS

WEEK 1 OBJECTIVES

_____
_____
_____
_____
_____

NEXT STEPS

OBSTACLES & SOLUTIONS

DEGREE OF PERSISTENCE

www.DrKesslyn.com

OIN ONLINE COMMUNITIES

Jan   Feb   Mar   April   May   June   July   Aug   Sept   Oct   Nov   Dec
3 4 5 6 7 8 9 10 11 12 13 14 15 16 17 18 19 20 21 22 23 24 25 26 27 28 29 30 31

REAM

TO DO

OALS

ACCOMPLISHMENTS

VEEK 1 OBJECTIVES

_____

_____

_____

_____

_____

NEXT STEPS

OBSTACLES & SOLUTIONS

DEGREE OF PERSISTENCE

KNOW YOURSELF

Jan	Feb	Mar	April	May	June	July	Aug	Sept	Oct	Nov	Dec
1 2 3	4 5 6	7 8 9	10 11 12	13 14 15	16 17 18	19 20	21 22 23	24 25 26	27 28	29 30	

DREAM

TO DO

GOALS

ACCOMPLISHMENTS

WEEK 1 OBJECTIVES

_____
_____
_____
_____
_____

NEXT STEPS

OBSTACLES & SOLUTIONS

DEGREE OF PERSISTENCE
www.DrKesslyn.com

LISTEN TO OTHERS

Jan   Feb   Mar   April   May   June   July   Aug   Sept   Oct   Nov   Dec
2 3 4 5 6 7 8 9 10 11 12 13 14 15 16 17 18 19 20 21 22 23 24 25 26 27 28 29 30 31

DREAM

TO DO

GOALS

ACCOMPLISHMENTS

WEEK 1 OBJECTIVES

_____

_____

_____

_____

_____

NEXT STEPS

OBSTACLES & SOLUTIONS

DEGREE OF PERSISTENCE
www.DrKesslyn.com

MANAGE EXPECTATIONS

Jan	Feb	Mar	April	May	June	July	Aug	Sept	Oct	Nov	Dec

1 2 3 4 5 6 7 8 9 10 11 12 13 14 15 16 17 18 19 20 21 22 23 24 25 26 27 28 29 30

DREAM

TO DO

GOALS

ACCOMPLISHMENTS

WEEK 1 OBJECTIVES

_____
_____
_____
_____
_____

NEXT STEPS

OBSTACLES & SOLUTIONS

DEGREE OF PERSISTENCE
www.DrKesslyn.com

NAVIGATE A NEW NORMAL

Jan   Feb   Mar   April   May   June   July   Aug   Sept   Oct   Nov   Dec
3 4 5 6 7 8 9 10 11 12 13 14 15 16 17 18 19 20 21 22 23 24 25 26 27 28 29 30 31

REAM

TO DO

OALS

ACCOMPLISHMENTS

VEEK 1 OBJECTIVES

_____

_____

_____

_____

NEXT STEPS

_____

OBSTACLES & SOLUTIONS

DEGREE OF PERSISTENCE
www.DrKesslyn.com

OPERATIONALIZE YOUR DREAM

Jan Feb Mar April May June July Aug Sept Oct Nov Dec
1 2 3 4 5 6 7 8 9 10 11 12 13 14 15 16 17 18 19 20 21 22 23 24 25 26 27 28 29 30

DREAM

TO DO

GOALS

ACCOMPLISHMENTS

WEEK 1 OBJECTIVES

_____

_____

_____

_____

NEXT STEPS

_____

OBSTACLES & SOLUTIONS

DEGREE OF PERSISTENCE

PRACTICE POSITIVE TALK

Jan	Feb	Mar	April	May	June	July	Aug	Sept	Oct	Nov	Dec

3 4 5 6 7 8 9 10 11 12 13 14 15 16 17 18 19 20 21 22 23 24 25 26 27 28 29 30 31

REAM

TO DO

OALS

ACCOMPLISHMENTS

VEEK 1 OBJECTIVES

_____

_____

_____

_____

_____

NEXT STEPS

OBSTACLES & SOLUTIONS

DEGREE OF PERSISTENCE

QUESTION EVERYTHING

Jan   Feb   Mar   April   May   June   July   Aug   Sept   Oct   Nov   Dec
1 2 3 4 5 6 7 8 9 10 11 12 13 14 15 16 17 18 19 20 21 22 23 24 25 26 27 28 29 30

DREAM

TO DO

GOALS

ACCOMPLISHMENTS

WEEK 1 OBJECTIVES

_____
_____
_____
_____
_____

NEXT STEPS

OBSTACLES & SOLUTIONS

DEGREE OF PERSISTENCE
www.DrKesslyn.com

RESPOND ACCORDINGLY

Jan   Feb   Mar   April   May   June   July   Aug   Sept   Oct   Nov   Dec
2 3 4 5 6 7 8 9 10 11 12 13 14 15 16 17 18 19 20 21 22 23 24 25 26 27 28 29 30 31

REAM

TO DO

GOALS

ACCOMPLISHMENTS

WEEK 1 OBJECTIVES

_____

_____

_____

_____

NEXT STEPS

_____

OBSTACLES & SOLUTIONS

DEGREE OF PERSISTENCE
www.DrKesslyn.com

SET YOUR ATMOSPHERE

Jan   Feb   Mar   April   May   June   July   Aug   Sept   Oct   Nov   Dec
1 2 3 4 5 6 7 8 9 10 11 12 13 14 15 16 17 18 19 20 21 22 23 24 25 26 27 28 29 30

DREAM

TO DO

GOALS

ACCOMPLISHMENTS

WEEK 1 OBJECTIVES

_____

_____

_____

_____

_____

NEXT STEPS

OBSTACLES & SOLUTIONS

DEGREE OF PERSISTENCE
www.DrKesslyn.com

RANSFORM INFORMATION INTO ACTION

Jan   Feb   Mar   April   May   June   July   Aug   Sept   Oct   Nov   Dec
3 4 5 6 7 8 9 10 11 12 13 14 15 16 17 18 19 20 21 22 23 24 25 26 27 28 29 30 31

REAM

TO DO

OALS

ACCOMPLISHMENTS

VEEK 1 OBJECTIVES

_____
_____
_____
_____
_____

NEXT STEPS

OBSTACLES & SOLUTIONS

DEGREE OF PERSISTENCE
www.DrKesslyn.com

UTILIZE YOUR RESOURCE

Jan   Feb   Mar   April   May   June   July   Aug   Sept   Oct   Nov   Dec
1 2 3 4 5 6 7 8 9 10 11 12 13 14 15 16 17 18 19 20 21 22 23 24 25 26 27 28 29 30

DREAM

TO DO

GOALS

ACCOMPLISHMENTS

WEEK 1 OBJECTIVES

_____
_____
_____
_____
_____

NEXT STEPS

OBSTACLES & SOLUTIONS

DEGREE OF PERSISTENCE
www.DrKesslyn.com

VALUE THE PROCESS

Jan   Feb   Mar   April   May   June   July   Aug   Sept   Oct   Nov   Dec
3 4 5 6 7 8 9 10 11 12 13 14 15 16 17 18 19 20 21 22 23 24 25 26 27 28 29 30 31

REAM

TO DO

OALS

ACCOMPLISHMENTS

VEEK 1 OBJECTIVES

_____

_____

_____

_____

NEXT STEPS

_____

OBSTACLES & SOLUTIONS

DEGREE OF PERSISTENCE
www.DrKesslyn.com

WEIGH THE COSTS

Jan Feb Mar April May June July Aug Sept Oct Nov Dec
1 2 3 4 5 6 7 8 9 10 11 12 13 14 15 16 17 18 19 20 21 22 23 24 25 26 27 28 29 30

DREAM

TO DO

GOALS

ACCOMPLISHMENTS

WEEK 1 OBJECTIVES

_____
_____
_____
_____
_____

NEXT STEPS

OBSTACLES & SOLUTIONS

DEGREE OF PERSISTENCE
www.DrKesslyn.com

K - OUT UNPRODUCTIVITY

Jan	Feb	Mar	April	May	June	July	Aug	Sept	Oct	Nov	Dec
3 4	5 6	7 8	9 10	11 12 13	14 15 16 17	18 19 20	21 22 23	24 25 26	27 28	29 30	31

REAM

TO DO

OALS

ACCOMPLISHMENTS

WEEK 1 OBJECTIVES

_____

_____

_____

_____

_____

NEXT STEPS

OBSTACLES & SOLUTIONS

DEGREE OF PERSISTENCE

YIELD TO THE PROCESS

Jan	Feb	Mar	April	May	June	July	Aug	Sept	Oct	Nov	Dec
1 2 3	4 5 6	7 8 9	10 11 12	13 14 15	16 17 18	19 20 21	22 23	24 25 26	27	28 29	30

DREAM

TO DO

GOALS

ACCOMPLISHMENTS

WEEK 1 OBJECTIVES

_____
_____
_____
_____
_____

NEXT STEPS

OBSTACLES & SOLUTIONS

DEGREE OF PERSISTENCE
www.DrKesslyn.com

ZERO IN ON OUTCOMES

Jan Feb Mar April May June July Aug Sept Oct Nov Dec
3 4 5 6 7 8 9 10 11 12 13 14 15 16 17 18 19 20 21 22 23 24 25 26 27 28 29 30 31

REAM

TO DO

OALS

ACCOMPLISHMENTS

EEK 1 OBJECTIVES

_____

_____

_____

_____

_____

NEXT STEPS

BSTACLES & SOLUTIONS

DEGREE OF PERSISTENCE
www.DrKesslyn.com

ACCEPT ACCOUNTABILIT

DREAM

TO DO

GOALS

ACCOMPLISHMENTS

WEEK 1 OBJECTIVES

_____
_____
_____
_____
_____

NEXT STEPS

OBSTACLES & SOLUTIONS

DEGREE OF PERSISTENCE

www.DrKesslyn.com

BE BOLD

REAM

TO DO

OALS

ACCOMPLISHMENTS

VEEK 1 OBJECTIVES

_____

_____

_____

_____

NEXT STEPS

_____

OBSTACLES & SOLUTIONS

DEGREE OF PERSISTENCE
www.DrKesslyn.com

CELEBRATE SMALL WINS

Jan   Feb   Mar   April   May   June   July   Aug   Sept   Oct   Nov   Dec
1 2 3 4 5 6 7 8 9 10 11 12 13 14 15 16 17 18 19 20 21 22 23 24 25 26 27 28 29 30

DREAM

TO DO

GOALS

ACCOMPLISHMENTS

WEEK 1 OBJECTIVES

_____
_____
_____
_____
_____

NEXT STEPS

OBSTACLES & SOLUTIONS

DEGREE OF PERSISTENCE
www.DrKesslyn.com

DISCIPLINE YOURSELF DAILY

Jan   Feb   Mar   April   May   June   July   Aug   Sept   Oct   Nov   Dec
3 4 5 6 7 8 9 10 11 12 13 14 15 16 17 18 19 20 21 22 23 24 25 26 27 28 29 30 31

REAM

TO DO

OALS

ACCOMPLISHMENTS

VEEK 1 OBJECTIVES

_____

_____

_____

_____   NEXT STEPS

_____

OBSTACLES & SOLUTIONS

DEGREE OF PERSISTENCE
www.DrKesslyn.com

EXAMINE YOUR STEPS

Jan	Feb	Mar	April	May	June	July	Aug	Sept	Oct	Nov	Dec
1 2 3	4 5 6	7 8 9	10 11 12	13 14 15	16 17 18	19 20 21	22 23	24 25 26	27	28 29	30

DREAM

TO DO

GOALS

ACCOMPLISHMENTS

WEEK 1 OBJECTIVES

_____
_____
_____
_____
_____

NEXT STEPS

OBSTACLES & SOLUTIONS

DEGREE OF PERSISTENCE
www.DrKesslyn.com

FOLLOW - UP

DREAM

TO DO

GOALS

ACCOMPLISHMENTS

WEEK 1 OBJECTIVES

_____

_____

_____

_____

_____

NEXT STEPS

OBSTACLES & SOLUTIONS

DEGREE OF PERSISTENCE
www.DrKesslyn.com

GET GUIDANCE

Jan Feb Mar April May June July Aug Sept Oct Nov Dec
1 2 3 4 5 6 7 8 9 10 11 12 13 14 15 16 17 18 19 20 21 22 23 24 25 26 27 28 29 30

DREAM

TO DO

GOALS

ACCOMPLISHMENTS

WEEK 1 OBJECTIVES

_____
_____
_____
_____
_____

NEXT STEPS

OBSTACLES & SOLUTIONS

DEGREE OF PERSISTENCE
www.DrKesslyn.com

HEED FEEDBACK

REAM

TO DO

OALS

ACCOMPLISHMENTS

WEEK 1 OBJECTIVES

_____

_____

_____

_____

NEXT STEPS

_____

OBSTACLES & SOLUTIONS

DEGREE OF PERSISTENCE

IMPLEMENT YOUR PLAN

Jan   Feb   Mar   April   May   June   July   Aug   Sept   Oct   Nov   Dec
1 2 3 4 5 6 7 8 9 10 11 12 13 14 15 16 17 18 19 20 21 22 23 24 25 26 27 28 29 30

DREAM

TO DO

GOALS

ACCOMPLISHMENTS

WEEK 1 OBJECTIVES

_____
_____
_____
_____
_____

NEXT STEPS

OBSTACLES & SOLUTIONS

DEGREE OF PERSISTENCE
www.DrKesslyn.com

JUST BE YOURSELF

Jan   Feb   Mar   April   May   June   July   Aug   Sept   Oct   Nov   Dec
3 4 5 6 7 8 9 10 11 12 13 14 15 16 17 18 19 20 21 22 23 24 25 26 27 28 29 30 31

REAM

TO DO

OALS

ACCOMPLISHMENTS

VEEK 1 OBJECTIVES

_____
_____
_____
_____
_____

NEXT STEPS

OBSTACLES & SOLUTIONS

DEGREE OF PERSISTENCE

KEEP GOING

DREAM

TO DO

GOALS

ACCOMPLISHMENTS

WEEK 1 OBJECTIVES

_____
_____
_____
_____
_____

NEXT STEPS

OBSTACLES & SOLUTIONS

DEGREE OF PERSISTENCE
www.DrKesslyn.com

LOSE THE ATTITUDE

Jan   Feb   Mar   April   May   June   July   Aug   Sept   Oct   Nov   Dec
3 4 5 6 7 8 9 10 11 12 13 14 15 16 17 18 19 20 21 22 23 24 25 26 27 28 29 30 31

REAM

TO DO

OALS

ACCOMPLISHMENTS

VEEK 1 OBJECTIVES

_____

_____

_____

_____

NEXT STEPS

_____

OBSTACLES & SOLUTIONS

DEGREE OF PERSISTENCE
www.DrKesslyn.com

MASTER MINDFULNESS

Jan   Feb   Mar   April   May   June   July   Aug   Sept   Oct   Nov   Dec
1 2 3 4 5 6 7 8 9 10 11 12 13 14 15 16 17 18 19 20 21 22 23 24 25 26 27 28 29 30

DREAM

TO DO

GOALS

ACCOMPLISHMENTS

WEEK 1 OBJECTIVES

_____
_____
_____
_____
_____

NEXT STEPS

OBSTACLES & SOLUTIONS

DEGREE OF PERSISTENCE
www.DrKesslyn.com

NEVER GIVE UP

Jan   Feb   Mar   April   May   June   July   Aug   Sept   Oct   Nov   Dec
3   4   5   6   7   8   9   10   11   12   13   14   15   16   17   18   19   20   21   22   23   24   25   26   27   28   29   30   31

DREAM

TO DO

GOALS

ACCOMPLISHMENTS

WEEK 1 OBJECTIVES

_____

_____

_____

_____

_____

NEXT STEPS

OBSTACLES & SOLUTIONS

DEGREE OF PERSISTENCE
www.DrKesslyn.com

OPTIMIZE YOUR STRENGTH

DREAM

TO DO

GOALS

ACCOMPLISHMENTS

WEEK 1 OBJECTIVES

_____

_____

_____

_____

NEXT STEPS

_____

OBSTACLES & SOLUTIONS

DEGREE OF PERSISTENCE

www.DrKesslyn.com

PERSIST

REAM

TO DO

OALS

ACCOMPLISHMENTS

WEEK 1 OBJECTIVES

_____

_____

_____

_____

_____

NEXT STEPS

_____

OBSTACLES & SOLUTIONS

DEGREE OF PERSISTENCE
www.DrKesslyn.com

QUANTIFY THE RESULTS

Jan	Feb	Mar	April	May	June	July	Aug	Sept	Oct	Nov	Dec

1 2 3 4 5 6 7 8 9 10 11 12 13 14 15 16 17 18 19 20 21 22 23 24 25 26 27 28 29 30

DREAM

TO DO

GOALS

ACCOMPLISHMENTS

WEEK 1 OBJECTIVES

_____
_____
_____
_____
_____

NEXT STEPS

OBSTACLES & SOLUTIONS

DEGREE OF PERSISTENCE
www.DrKesslyn.com

REFLECT ON YOUR "WHY"

Jan   Feb   Mar   April   May   June   July   Aug   Sept   Oct   Nov   Dec

3 4 5 6 7 8 9 10 11 12 13 14 15 16 17 18 19 20 21 22 23 24 25 26 27 28 29 30 31

REAM

TO DO

OALS

ACCOMPLISHMENTS

VEEK 1 OBJECTIVES

_____

_____

_____

_____

_____

NEXT STEPS

OBSTACLES & SOLUTIONS

DEGREE OF PERSISTENCE
www.DrKesslyn.com

SHATTER GLASS CEILING:

| Jan | Feb | Mar | April | May | June | July | Aug | Sept | Oct | Nov | Dec |

1 2 3 4 5 6 7 8 9 10 11 12 13 14 15 16 17 18 19 20 21 22 23 24 25 26 27 28 29 30

DREAM

TO DO

GOALS

ACCOMPLISHMENTS

WEEK 1 OBJECTIVES

_____
_____
_____
_____
_____

NEXT STEPS

OBSTACLES & SOLUTIONS

DEGREE OF PERSISTENCE

THINK OUTSIDE THE BOX

Jan	Feb	Mar	April	May	June	July	Aug	Sept	Oct	Nov	Dec

3 4 5 6 7 8 9 10 11 12 13 14 15 16 17 18 19 20 21 22 23 24 25 26 27 28 29 30 31

DREAM

TO DO

GOALS

ACCOMPLISHMENTS

WEEK 1 OBJECTIVES

_____

_____

_____

_____

_____

NEXT STEPS

OBSTACLES & SOLUTIONS

DEGREE OF PERSISTENCE

www.DrKesslyn.com

UNDERSTAND THE PROCES

Jan	Feb	Mar	April	May	June	July	Aug	Sept	Oct	Nov	Dec

1 2 3 4 5 6 7 8 9 10 11 12 13 14 15 16 17 18 19 20 21 22 23 24 25 26 27 28 29 30

DREAM

TO DO

GOALS

ACCOMPLISHMENTS

WEEK 1 OBJECTIVES

_____

_____

_____

_____

_____

NEXT STEPS

OBSTACLES & SOLUTIONS

DEGREE OF PERSISTENCE
www.DrKesslyn.com

VALUE YOURSELF

REAM

TO DO

OALS

ACCOMPLISHMENTS

WEEK 1 OBJECTIVES

_____

_____

_____

_____   NEXT STEPS

_____

OBSTACLES & SOLUTIONS

DEGREE OF PERSISTENCE
www.DrKesslyn.com

WALK IN TRUTH

Jan	Feb	Mar	April	May	June	July	Aug	Sept	Oct	Nov	Dec

1 2 3 4 5 6 7 8 9 10 11 12 13 14 15 16 17 18 19 20 21 22 23 24 25 26 27 28 29 30

DREAM

TO DO

GOALS

ACCOMPLISHMENTS

WEEK 1 OBJECTIVES

_____

_____

_____

_____

_____

NEXT STEPS

OBSTACLES & SOLUTIONS

DEGREE OF PERSISTENCE
www.DrKesslyn.com

X-RAY THE RESULTS

REAM

TO DO

OALS

ACCOMPLISHMENTS

EEK 1 OBJECTIVES

_____

_____

_____

_____

NEXT STEPS

BSTACLES & SOLUTIONS

YEARN FOR COMPLETION

Jan	Feb	Mar	April	May	June	July	Aug	Sept	Oct	Nov	Dec
1 2 3	4 5 6	7 8 9	10 11 12	13 14 15	16 17 18	19 20 21	22 23 24	25 26	27	28 29	30

DREAM

TO DO

GOALS

ACCOMPLISHMENTS

WEEK 1 OBJECTIVES

_____
_____
_____
_____
_____

NEXT STEPS

OBSTACLES & SOLUTIONS

DEGREE OF PERSISTENCE
www.DrKesslyn.com

ZOOM TOWARD THE CELEBRATION

REAM

TO DO

OALS

ACCOMPLISHMENTS

VEEK 1 OBJECTIVES

_____

_____

_____

_____

_____

NEXT STEPS

BSTACLES & SOLUTIONS

DEGREE OF PERSISTENCE
www.DrKesslyn.com

Conclusion

There was a significant amount of practical advice within these pages. I hope that this short, easy read provided you with some helpful hints for addressing the mental, emotional, financial, logistical, and relational issues that surface for many doctoral pursuers. I believe that these tips will support you, no matter where you are along the journey.

Know that you have people at The PhD Consultants who understand the journey and are poised to help you reach your doctoral goals. For ongoing support, reach out to learn more about me and the services that are provided by The PhD Consultants. We look forward to helping you persist so that you can make an even greater dynamic difference in the world.

"I help doctoral pursuers become doctoral achievers so they can leverage their educational research to make a dynamic difference in the world."

To learn more, visit:

www.DrKesslyn.com

www.ThePhDConsultants.com

CPSIA information can be obtained
at www.ICGtesting.com
Printed in the USA
BVHW041046191221
624455BV00017B/1494